First World War
and Army of Occupation
War Diary
France, Belgium and Germany

66 DIVISION
197 Infantry Brigade
Lancashire Fusiliers
3/5th (T) Battalion
1 September 1915 - 5 February 1916

WO95/3137/1

The Naval & Military Press Ltd
www.nmarchive.com
Published in association with The National Archives

Published by

The Naval & Military Press Ltd

Unit 10 Ridgewood Industrial Park,

Uckfield, East Sussex,

TN22 5QE England

Tel: +44 (0) 1825 749494

www.naval-military-press.com

www.nmarchive.com

This diary has been reprinted in facsimile from the original. Any imperfections are inevitably reproduced and the quality may fall short of modern type and cartographic standards.

© **Crown Copyright**
Images reproduced by permission of The National Archives, London, England, 2015.

Contents

Document type	Place/Title	Date From	Date To
Heading	66th Division 197th Infy Bde 3-5th Bn Lancs Fus. 1915 Sep-1916 Feb 1917 Feb-1918 Feb		
Heading	WO95/3137/1		
Heading	66 Div 197 Bde 3/5 Bn Lancs Fus 1915 Sep-1916 Feb		
Heading	War Diary of 3/5th Lancashire Fusiliers From February 1st To 29th February 1916 Volume I		
Miscellaneous	War Diary Statement		
War Diary	Crowborough	01/09/1915	21/10/1915
War Diary	Tunbridge Wells	22/10/1915	27/01/1916
War Diary	Hartfield	02/02/1916	02/02/1916
War Diary	Tunbridge Wells	05/02/1916	05/02/1916

66TH DIVISION
197TH INFY BDE

3-5TH BN LANCS FUS.
~~FAR 1917 FEB 1918~~

1915 SEP — 1916 FEB
1917 FEB — 1918 FEB

DISBANDED

WO 95/31371

66 DIV

197 BDE

3/5 BN LANCS FUS

1915 SEP — 1916 FEB

8024

CONFIDENTIAL

WAR=DIARY

of

3/5th LANCASHIRE FUSILIERS

FROM February 1st to 29th February 1916.

VOLUME I

****

Army Form C. 2118

WAR DIARY Statement
or
INTELLIGENCE SUMMARY
(Erase heading not required.)

Instructions regarding War Diaries and Intelligence Summaries are contained in F.S. Regs., Part II. and the Staff Manual respectively. Title Pages will be prepared in manuscript.

Place	Date	Hour	Summary of Events and Information	Remarks and references to Appendices
			UNIT 3/5th. Battalion Lancashire Fusiliers.	
			BRIGADE 197th. Infantry Brigade.	
			DIVISION 66th. (East Lancashire) Division.	
			MOBILIZATION CENTRE Bury.	
			TEMPORARY STATION Crowborough.	
			STATIONS SINCE OCCUPIED SUBSEQUENT TO xxxxxx CONCENTRATION Southport and Maidstone.	
			(a) MOBILIZATION Nil	
			(b) CONCENTRATION AT WAR STATION.	
			(c) ORGANISATION FOR DEFENCE	
			(d) TRAINING This Battalion has 200 Japanese Rifles. There are no other arms and consequently 80 men are unarmed. There is no ammunition column. Elementary Training was progressing up to the 9th. On that date the Battalion moved to Maidstone and was engaged on trench digging at Cossington Fields. Instruction received very good. N.C.O's are new men and as such are being trained in their duties and have shewn improvement.	

1875 Wt. W593/826 1,000,000 4/15 J.B.C. & A. A.D.S.S./Forms/C. 2118.

WAR DIARY
or
INTELLIGENCE SUMMARY

(Erase heading not required.)

Army Form C. 2118

Place	Date	Hour	Summary of Events and Information	Remarks and references to Appendices
			(f) ADMINISTRATION	
			1. Medical Services There is no M.O. attached to this Unit.	
			2. Veterinary Services.	
			3. Supply Services.	
			4. Transport Services. 11 Draught Horses 9 Pack Mules, 1 four-wheeled lorry 1 two-wheeled Cart and 3 Limbered Wagons G.S.	
			5. Ordnance Services	
			6. Billeting The Battalion was billeted without subsistence in Maidstone from 9th. to 30th. at 9d. per man per night. The Technical Advance Party, 1 officer and 8 men were billeted with subsistence.	
			7. Channels of correspondence No change.	
			8. Range construction	
			9. Supply of Remounts.	
			(g) RE-ORGANISATION INTO HOME AND IMPERIAL SERVICE.	
			(h) PREPARATION INTO UNITS FOR IMPERIAL SERVICE.	

Godfrey Major.

Commanding 3/5th. Battalion Lancashire Fusiliers.

Army Form C. 2118

WAR DIARY
or
INTELLIGENCE SUMMARY

(Erase heading not required.)

Instructions regarding War Diaries and Intelligence Summaries are contained in F. S. Regs., Part II. and the Staff Manual respectively. Title Pages will be prepared in manuscript.

197/60

Place	Date	Hour	Summary of Events and Information	Remarks and references to Appendices
Crowborough.				
	1-9-15		2nd. Lieut. N.D.Thompson appointed Battalion Machine Gun Officer.	
	3-9-15		62 N.C.O's and men attended "B" Range to fire Japanese Musketry Course.	
	3-9-15		1 Officer 10 men detailed for Bomb-throwing Instruction under 2nd. Lt. McCulloch 2/6th. Battn. Lancashire Fusiliers.	
	10-9-15		Instructional Court Martials and Examination of Officers on King's Regulations and Manual of Military Law weekly commenced.	
	13-9-15		2nd. Lieut. C.G.Lang (9th. King's Own Scottish Borderers) reported for duty.	
	15-9-15		Inspection by Lieut-General C.L.Woollcombe C.B.	
	15-9-15		2nd. Lieut. A.D.Blades reported for duty.	
	17-9-15		Inspection by Colonel A.A.Garstin C.M.G. of Battalion at Bayonet Fighting.	
	17-9-15		Battalion was detailed for Divisional Duties	
	20-9-15		3443 Pte.F.Clegg discharged as no longer physically fit for war service.	
	20-9-15		2nd. Lieuts.Cowan, Higgins, Horne, Rae, Reid (9th. King's Own Scottish Borderers) reported for duty.	
	22-9-15		2nd. Lieuts.Cowan & Higgins transferred to 2/6th. Battalion Lancashire Fusiliers.	
			2nd. Lieuts.Horne & Rae transferred to 2/7th. Battalion Lancashire Fusiliers.	
			2nd. Lieuts. Lang & Reid transferred to 2/8th. Battalion Lancashire Fusiliers.	
	28-9-15		Inspection of Transport by Brigadier-General C.E.Beckett C.B.	
			Battalion engaged on Musketry Instruction.	

Geo A Kay Major.

Commanding 3/5th. Battalion Lancashire Fusiliers.

Army Form C. 2118

WAR DIARY
or
INTELLIGENCE SUMMARY

(Erase heading not required.)

Instructions regarding War Diaries and Intelligence Summaries are contained in F.S. Regs., Part II. and the Staff Manual respectively. Title Pages will be prepared in manuscript.

Place	Date	Hour	Summary of Events and Information	Remarks and references to Appendices
Crowborough. Tunbridge Wells.	7-10-15		Brigade Bivouaced at Gills Lap. Scheme of Outposts. Battalion held in reserve.	
	8-10-15		3502 Cpl. Simpkin M. and 2877 Pte Bradshaw W. discharged as being no longer physically fit for war service.	CWM
	13-10-15		Inspection of Transport by Brigadier-General Beckett C.B.	
	21-10-15		Marched from Crowborough to Tunbridge Wells to take up quarters in billets.	
Tunbridge Wells.	22-10-15		3592 L/Cpl. Senorian N. discharged as being no longer physically fit for war service.	CWM
	30-10-15		Hon. Lieut. & Quartermaster H. Rice placed under open arrest on a charge of conduct to the prejudice of good order and Military discipline	

Geo A Key Major.

Commanding 3/5th. Battalion Lancashire Fusiliers.

ing
WAR DIARY

INTELLIGENCE SUMMARY

(Erase heading not required.)

Army Form C. 2118

197/66

Place	Date	Hour	Summary of Events and Information	Remarks and references to Appendices
Tunbridge Wells	9/11/15	9 a.m.	Lieut-Colonel John Hall V.D. assumed command of the Battalion. Strength 12 Officers 23 attached Officers and 275 other ranks reg.	
"	16/11/15	10.45 a.m.	Inspection by Major General Pickson Inspector General of Infantry. Men employed on duties carried on practice in Arms Drill. All duty men detailed to attend. 2 Parades a week reg.	
"	23/11/15	11 a.m.	Received from C.O.O. Weedon 540 C.L.L.E. Rifles and 525 Bayonets reg.	
"	"	1.45 p.m.	Despatched to C.O.O. Weedon 14,000 rounds Japanese ammunition 259 Japanese Rifles 255 Bayonets 155 Bags 170 Bottles Oil 219 Cleaning Buckets 213 Screwdrivers 5 Dickinson Platforms reg.	
"	24/11/15	10 a.m.	Inspection of Brigade by Brigadier Colonel A.H. Paxton C.M.G. Each of Recruits with no arms in firing and unfixing bayonets. Arms Drill daily for all men other than recruits not yet issued with rifles reg.	

JH Hall
Lt-Col
Commanding 38 Batt Lanc Fus.

Army Form C. 2118

107/60

WAR DIARY

INTELLIGENCE SUMMARY

(Erase heading not required.)

Instructions regarding War Diaries and Intelligence Summaries are contained in F. S. Regs., Part II. and the Staff Manual respectively. Title Pages will be prepared in manuscript.

Place	Date	Hour	Summary of Events and Information	Remarks and references to Appendices
Tunbridge Wells	10/12/15	2.30 P.M.	The Brigade was inspected by O.C. 66th (East Lancs) Division. KSS.	
"	19/12/15	2. P.M	Transferred temporarily to C.R.A 66th / East Lancs/ Divisional R.F.A 48 Rifles .303 and 20 rounds of ammunition per rifle. KSS.	
"	19/12/15	10 A.M.	Transferred 82 Recruits from 2/6 th Battn Lanc Fusiliers KSS.	
"	21/12/15	10 A.M.	Transferred 15 Rifles to C.O.O. Weedon KSS.	

J W Hall Lt=Col
Commanding 3/5th Battn Lanc Fus.

Army Form C. 2118

WAR DIARY
or
INTELLIGENCE SUMMARY
(Erase heading not required.)

Instructions regarding War Diaries and Intelligence Summaries are contained in F. S. Regs., Part II. and the Staff Manual respectively. Title Pages will be prepared in manuscript.

197/60

Place	Date	Hour	Summary of Events and Information	Remarks and references to Appendices
Tunbridge Wells.	27-1-16	11 A:M	Inspection of Battalion at work on Upper Cricket Ground and of Battalion billets, by Lieut-General Sir Charles L. Woollcombe K.C.B. Commanding 2nd. Army, Central Force.	

John Hall Lt-Colonel.
Commanding 3/5th. Batt. Lanc. Fusiliers.

Army Form C. 2118

WAR DIARY ~~INTELLIGENCE SUMMARY~~

(Erase heading not required.)

Instructions regarding War Diaries and Intelligence Summaries are contained in F. S. Regs., Part II. and the Staff Manual respectively. Title Pages will be prepared in manuscript.

Place	Date	Hour	Summary of Events and Information	Remarks and references to Appendices
Hartfield.	2/2/16.	12 noon.	Divisional Transport Concentration March. 1st Line transport and Field ambulance.	
Tunbridge Wells.	5/2/16.		No 3496 Private T. Meadowcroft died in the City of London General Hospital Chelsea.	

John Hair Lt-Colonel.
Commanding 3/5th Batt. Lancashire Fusiliers.

www.ingramcontent.com/pod-product-compliance
Lightning Source LLC
Chambersburg PA
CBHW081517160426
43193CB00014B/2721